W9-BUZ-068

DATE DUE

#47-0108 Peel Off Pressure Sensitive

GEORGE HERBERT WALKER BUSH

A Photographic Profile

COMPILED BY

David Valdez

Texas A&M University Press
COLLEGE STATION

All photographs courtesy of the White House.

Publication of this volume is made possible by a generous grant from
MBNA Corporation and the Cawley Family
in cooperation with
the George Bush Presidential Library Foundation.

The paper used in this book meets the minimum requirements
of the American National Standard for Permanence
of Paper for Printed Library Materials, Z39.48-1984.
Binding materials have been chosen for durability.

Library of Congress Cataloging-in-Publication Data

Valdez, David, 1949–
    George Herbert Walker Bush : a photographic profile / compiled
by David Valdez.—1st ed.
        p.   cm.
    ISBN 0-89096-779-2 (alk. paper)
    1. Bush, George, 1924–   —Pictorial works. 2. Presidents—
United States—Pictorial works.   I. Title.
E882.V35   1997   97-9566
973.928'092—dc21   CIP

To Sarah Jane,

my life's partner

Without her help, support,

& understanding,

this book would not have been possible

Contents

Introduction

I had always planned to do a book, but not until the end of President Bush's second term in office. When the election did not go the way we had planned, I knew a new life was about to begin for all concerned. The famous Disney commercial, "What are you going to do now that you have won the Super Bowl?" never had more meaning to me than at that moment. A few months after the election, I was on my way to Walt Disney World to begin a whole new, exciting career.

After some initial adjustment to life in Florida, I thought it was time to get started on this book. As I was sorting through the thousands of images, I relived the many memories and realized again what a privilege and honor it had been to work not only for the vice president but also for the president of the United States.

The highest honor for me during the nine years of working for President George Bush was for him to introduce me as his friend. I would always address him as Mr. President throughout our working relationship and thought of him only in those terms. This became quite evident one morning at Walker's Point in Kennebunkport when Mrs. Bush came out of their bedroom and asked me

if I had seen George. George? George? Who was this George? Not a staffer. Not Secret Service. She realized I had no clue who she was talking about and said, "You know the president of the United States." It is this type of memory that the photographs in this book will evoke in those who have worked with the Bushes over the years. And for those who know them only from their public life, this book will hopefully provide a little more insight into the life of George Herbert Walker Bush.

The book is divided into three sections, The Early Years, The Vice Presidency, and The Presidency. The black-and-white photographs of the early years were the first photos I saw when I began working for then Vice President Bush. They taught me a little about this man I would be spending so much time with in the next nine years.

In December, 1983, when on assignment for *Nations Business* magazine to shoot the topping of the National Christmas Tree by Barbara Bush, Scott Applewhite (Associated Press photographer) told me that Vice President Bush had an opening for a staff photographer.

There was no doubt that I would send a resumé, but to whom?

Research led me to Shirley Green, the acting press secretary to the vice president. Shirley called me in for an interview and back again for a second interview with Adm. Dan Murphy, chief of staff. The interview with the admiral was the toughest interview this Texan had ever been through, and I was sure when I left his office no job would come of it. But surprisingly, within days there was a call to come in and meet Mr. Bush.

The first person to greet me was Susie Peake, the vice president's assistant. "The vice president will see you now," Susie said as she escorted me in. The interview of my life was about to begin with one of the most gracious, kind, and gentle people I have ever known. Vice President Bush greeted me and put me at ease immediately. I was to see him do this so many times with world leaders, friends, and colleagues. He showed me his office and photographs of his family, who were obviously very important to him. He knew more than I did how much time I would spend not only with him but with the entire Bush family, and he was getting me acquainted right at the start. I later learned the Bush family extends beyond blood relatives to people like Shirley Green, Don Rhodes, Jack Steel, Rose Zameria, and Patty Presock. These folks taught me more about the man I was to work for than those black-and-white photos that I studied so much in my first days.

History was in the making and my camera was there to record a unique period in world history. During his vice presidency, we traveled to Poland to meet a shipyard worker who predicted Poland would be free and George Bush would be president of the United States. We returned to a free Poland, and President George Bush met with the newly elected President Lech Wałesa with a million cheering, free Polish people looking on.

An experience that haunts me today and will until I die is the visit to Auschwitz. I remember being escorted on a tour of the Nazi concentration camps and feeling like I had stepped into the gates of hell. I had nightmares for a long time after that visit and I know it had a profound effect on the man George Bush.

In 1984 when Ronald Reagan and George Bush were running for reelection, Geraldine Ferraro was picked by Walter Mondale to be his running mate. The conversations and concern about how to treat her in the debate were incredible. As it turned out, she was the vice presidential candidate and it did not matter if she were a woman or not. The vice president treated her as the competitor she was and the next day the *New York Post* headlines declared "George Wins One for the Gipper."

Life magazine put in a request to spend time with the Bush family in Kennebunkport one summer, but the family did not want some strange photographer around, so I was given the assignment. One of the photographs I took of the Bushes in bed with some of the grandchildren ran two full pages in *Life* and, consequently, was published worldwide. That photo continues to be published all these many years later.

I remember flying to Indiana in 1986 to cover a campaign for Dan Quayle who was running for the United States Senate. He was a fine, young, good-looking man who was full of energy and enthusiasm. To me it was no surprise in August of 1988 in New Orleans at the Republican National Convention that Senator Quayle was chosen to be the vice presidential nominee. The first few minutes after he arrived to meet with Vice President Bush and Jim Baker, I found myself alone with Senator Quayle and his wife, Marilyn, in the hotel where we were staying. The adrenalin was high and I found myself making small talk, trying to make them comfortable. It was an exciting moment in the political process and a moment few people ever find themselves in, being selected to become vice president of the United States. I consider Vice President Quayle a friend and I know he contributed greatly to the Bush presidency.

The day after the election we returned to Washington, D.C., and went back to work. On the day of the inauguration, it was hard to find President-Elect Bush alone at the Blair House, the guesthouse of the President, but I finally did at the moment when the vice president was practicing his inaugural address. The entire Bush family was around and toys were everywhere. It reminded me of any typical American family, but this family was moments away from becoming the First Family of the United States of America.

When George Bush was a senior at Yale, he had an opportunity to meet Babe Ruth as the "Babe" presented his original manuscript of his autobiography to the university. President Bush, who jokingly referred to himself as the world's greatest name dropper, had a chance as president to invite anyone he wanted to the White House. I almost always overcame the urge to ask for a celebrity's autograph, but when Ted Williams and Joe DiMaggio were guests, a moment of weakness fell over me and I obtained an autographed baseball signed by both of these baseball greats.

Another awe inspiring sporting moment in history took place at Camp David on a visit by President Gorbachev of the Soviet Union. The two presidents were busy in their meetings when they decided to take a break. President Gorbachev went for a walk. I couldn't resist the moment to photograph him, so I went along. It was always my position not to get involved in any activity I was photographing, yet this was an unusual situation. President Gorbachev came upon the famous Camp David horseshoe pits and was curious, so I showed him how to play. With the grace of a Russian ballet dancer, President Gorbachev threw a ringer on his first throw. He walked off the pits with the shoe and later that night explained how in the Soviet Union the horseshoe was a symbol of good luck.

On December 25, 1991, when President Gorbachev resigned and the Soviet Union disappeared, I wondered how his good luck was holding up. In 1995 former President Bush met with former President Gorbachev in Colorado. They were both well.

No president wants a war and President Bush having been in combat, experiencing the death of his crew members, would be at the top of the list when it comes to staying out of war. When international law was violated and a person such as Gen. Manuel Noriega was in a position of participating in the promotion of the distribution of drugs, President Bush acted swiftly and courageously to protect the integrity of the Panama Canal and to bring General Noriega to justice. A truth about war is that people are harmed. As President Bush visited with the injured troops in San Antonio, Texas, nothing could have been more moving when an injured soldier presented Mr. Bush a tiny American flag and said thank you for fighting for democracy. That flag remained on the president's desk in the Oval Office until January 20, 1993.

On the international front so many things happened during the Reagan/Bush presidencies that it will be written about for years to come. On March 11, 1985, Mikhail Gorbachev was named general secretary of the Communist party of the Soviet Union. By 1986, Mr. Gorbachev called for "radical reform" of the Soviet economy setting the stage for unexpected events. In 1987, he called for political reform and multi-candidate elections. President Ronald Reagan and General Secretary Mikhail Gorbachev in December, 1987, signed a treaty banning medium-range nuclear missiles. In March, 1989, George Bush had been president for less than three months when the Communist party in Poland approved solidarity's inclusion in elections, ending a forty-five-year monopoly on power. That May, Hungary pulled down the barbed wire fence along its border with Austria, making Hungary the first Eastern European country with an open border to Western Europe. On February 25, 1989, President Bush visited the People's Republic of China, and on June 4, 1989, students demonstrated for freedom and democracy in Tiananmen Square in the People's Republic of China. That same day Polish Communists were defeated in national elections. November 9, 1989, was the destruction of the Berlin Wall. In December of that year Romanian leader Nicolae Ceauşescu and his wife were executed and Václav Havel was elected president of the Czechoslovak parliament. In February, 1990, President Bush and German Chancellor Helmut Kohl met to discuss the unification of Germany. On May 29, 1990, Boris Yeltsin was elected parliamentary leader of the Russian Republic, in effect the new Russian president.

Iraq invaded Kuwait on August 2, 1990. In September, President Bush and Mr. Gorbachev met in Helsinki to discuss the Persian Gulf crisis and agreed to hold a Middle East peace conference. On October 3, 1990, the Germanies reunited. That December, Lech Walesa was elected president of a free Poland, as he had predicted to Vice President Bush many years previous. On January 16 the Persian Gulf war began and by February 23 President Bush announced that Kuwait was liberated. August brought a coup attempt against Gorbachev and he resigned from the Communist party. The Soviet parliament banned Communist party activities. On December 25 Gorbachev resigned and the Soviet Union disappeared.

President Bush always struck me as a compassionate man who worked for the underdog but was reluctant to receive praise for his efforts. He had been the leader of the United Negro College Fund drive on the Yale campus in 1948. It was that involvement that made it difficult for him to understand why twenty years later when he was a U.S. congressman he was booed and given catcalls by his constitu-

ents for advocating open housing. One of the proudest moments in his public career was convincing an angry crowd that fair and open housing was a fundamental right for all.

President Bush had a great opportunity to help another group of Americans who had been left behind. At the signing ceremony of the Americans with Disabilities Act on the South Lawn of the White House, President Bush said, "This historic act is the world's first comprehensive declaration of equality for people with disabilities—the first. Its passage has made the United States the international leader on this human rights issue. This act is powerful in its simplicity. It will ensure that people with disabilities are given the basic guarantees for which they have worked so long and so hard: independence, freedom of choice, control of their lives, the opportunity to blend fully and equally into the rich mosaic of the American mainstream."

Other domestic achievements of President Bush's administration included passage of the Clean Air Act, the signing of the Civil Rights Act of 1991, the signing of the North American Free Trade Agreement, and the enactment of the surface transportation legislation, a bill that authorized $151 billion for highway construction, safety, and transit spending.

The president called himself the education president and one of the first things he did in office was to hold an education summit. Governors were invited. The governor of Arkansas was there and prominently photographed. Who was that guy? History would play that one out when I photographed President-Elect Clinton with President Bush in the fall of 1992.

Being a part of history as it happens, you do not appreciate what is occurring until you are separated from the day-to-day routine of White House meetings with the cabinet, senators, representatives of Congress, never ending trips and unscheduled events. A photograph was made of the new presidential cabinet. Included in this cabinet photo was Senator John Tower, the secretary of defense nominee. As it turned out, Richard Cheney was selected as the secretary of defense, so a new photograph had to be taken. This was the only time a second chance was given to take another photograph. Photographers can painfully remember President Bush giving only seconds of his time to pose for a photograph. This book is an attempt to capture in photographs and in his personal quotes the life of George Herbert Walker Bush, a man uniquely qualified to be the forty-first president of the United States.

Born in Milton, Massachusetts on June 12, 1924, he was destined to live in a world that was about to go to war. Before his nineteenth birthday, after graduating from Phillips Academy, he went into the navy and became the youngest navy fighter pilot of his time. He was tested in battle and was awarded the Distinguished Flying Cross for his service. When he finished his tour in 1945, it was time to attend Yale where he graduated Phi Beta Kappa. It was during this time that Barbara Pierce became Barbara Bush and the new family moved to Texas to enter the oil business. Many jobs were to follow: from congressman in 1966 and ambassador to the United Nations in 1971, to chairman of the Republican National Committee in 1973 and chief of the United States Liaison Office in the People's Republic of China in 1974. He also held the position of director of the Central Intelligence Agency in 1976.

In 1979, George Bush decided it was time to run for president, yet there was one obstacle, Ronald Reagan. By 1980, Reagan had asked Bush to be his vice presidential running mate and they were elected to office. It was not until 1984 that I had the chance to work for their administration. In November, 1989, President-Elect George Bush invited me to be a part of his administration as the director of the White House Photo Office and his personal photographer.

Even though I had worked for the vice president for five years, I was still not prepared to be working for the president of the United States. I was in total awe of the office. But I saw quickly that President Bush felt the same about the presidency and was ever mindful of his stewardship and responsibilities as president. It was fun to be with him when he would turn to me or other staffers and comment how neat it was to be in the Kremlin or boating with King Hussein. When the president went into the Oval Office, he put on his suit jacket, as we all did, out of respect for the office and what it represented, no matter what the situation.

Integrity and class would be two of many adjectives I would use to describe the man that allowed me complete access to his public and private life. I hope that the photographs that my staff, Susan Biddle, Carol Powers, Joyce Naltchayan, and I took are able to depict what I was privileged to experience every day.

The Bush family was large by most standards yet on a visit to Kingsville, Texas, home to the Valdez family, I had an opportunity to have a small portion of my family photographed with President Bush. The White House staff was so overwhelmed by my definition of small—we needed our own separate holding room. Thank you President Bush for taking more than a second with my family.

Since leaving office, President Bush has devoted his time and energy in a number of directions. The central focus of his efforts has been the completion of the George Bush Presidential Library, which is located on the campus of Texas A&M University in College Station, Texas. Mr. Bush is also the chairman of the Eisenhower Exchange Fellowship, and he serves on the Board of Visitors of the M.D. Anderson Cancer Center in Houston, Texas. In all, President and Mrs. Bush have helped to support more than a hundred charitable organizations in their community and around the country from fighting drug abuse to promoting literacy.

President Bush has been the recipient of many honorary degrees, and he has received high honors from such countries as Kuwait, the United Kingdom, the Federal Republic of Germany, Nicaragua, Poland, and Albania.

Many people helped me with this book, but without the love and encouragement of my dear wife, Sarah Jane, none of this would have been possible. Her support during the years I was away more than I was home can never be repaid. But with her love and the love of the Lord, we have grown closer through this experience and look back with fond memories of the Bush family, Kennebunkport, Camp David, and White House Christmas parties. I also want to acknowledge her with developing the original design concept of this book.

George Bush Presidential Library groundbreaking ceremony, Texas A&M University, College Station, Texas

I want it clearly understood that Shirley Green was the person who hired me, and I will forever be grateful to her for giving me the opportunity to work for the president of the United States. Thank you Shirley.

Patty Presock made the access to the president possible by fully understanding the need to document the presidency and I thank her for that trust. Patty was responsible for keeping me fully informed during Desert Storm. The off-the-record briefings by Secretary Dick Cheney and Gen. Colin Powell were vital parts of the recorded history, and it will always be there for people to study. Patty also was sensitive to the private family moments and kept me in the loop. Many great photographs of the personal side of the family were made, and even today, when I show people, the response is always surprise that this president was so at ease with himself and others. I always maintained that if every American could have witnessed what I did, George Bush would have been reelected. But life goes on and the Bush family is happy to have more time together.

The U.S. Secret Service are the best people in the world under the extreme pressure they have to live with minute by minute. I appreciate their efforts and the service they provide to the United States.

The White House Communications Agency is the most professional group I have ever had the privilege to work with and they were right when they said I would miss them. I do. Thank you for the great work.

Without Billy Dale and the rest of the former White House Travel Office, I never would have found a single bag, camera, or roll of film. Miss you guys.

John Keller. He is the best of the best from the Advance Office.

John Sununu opened his home to Vice President Bush and George Bush came out the president. Thank you John.

Andy Card kept us all sane with his levelheadedness and should be president of the United States some day.

Tim McBride is a friend, and as described by Mrs. Bush is "one of the finest young men we know." Tim was with me through many of the good vice presidency days and the presidency. I thank him for his loyalty to the president and to me as a friend.

Marlin Fitzwater and I enjoyed many times together and I want him to know I appreciate the trust he placed in me and the guidance he gave me in getting the right photographs to the press.

Susan Biddle was my associate who worked every assignment with me and always came away with very moving, emotional photographs, many featured in this book.

Carol Powers, Mrs. Bush's photographer, added the necessary balance to the total coverage of the presidency and I thank her for her support.

Joyce Naltchayan came to me as an intern during the vice presidency and she grew into an excellent photographer during the presidency. I thank her for her loyalty, trust, and continued friendship.

Thank you President Bush and Vic Gold, author of the president's biography, *Looking Forward,* for allowing me to use selected quotes in this book.

Thanks to Eastman Kodak Company, the George Bush Presidential Library Foundation, Virginia Nell Beavers, Don Wilson, Michael Dannehauer, David Alsobrook, Kathy Super, Mary Finch, and the staff at Texas A&M University Press.

There are too many to thank for working with me and making my life during that time much easier. I could go on, but I would never finish. Those on the White House staff who kept me encouraged, entertained, and provided a camaraderie, they will always be remembered and cherished.

The political people that sacrifice and support their candidates are the true heroes that make the entire system work.

The desire for this book is to bring back memories for some, but for most it is to show a little of what goes on behind the scenes and more importantly, the personal side of President George Herbert Walker Bush. My position allowed me to be a recorder of history, and the president was always mindful of history and in the close of his inaugural address he said, "Some see leadership as high drama and the sound of trumpets calling, and sometimes it is that. But I see history as a book with many pages, and each day we fill a page with acts of hopefulness and meaning. The new breeze blows, a page turns, the story unfolds. And so, today, a chapter begins, a small and stately story of unity, diversity, and generosity-shared and written, together. Thank you. God Bless you. And God bless the United States of America."

Thank you President Bush for allowing me to record that history.

David Valdez

THE EARLY YEARS

1924–1980

Grandfather Walker was born into a devout Catholic family in St. Louis and named after the seventeenth-century religious poet George Herbert. He was a midwestern businessman, but more of a free spirited entrepreneur than my Ohio grandfather, Sam Bush. I was named after my grandfather George Herbert Walker. My mother couldn't make up her mind which of her father's names she wanted me to have, George Walker or Herbert Walker. When christening time arrived, she finally decided not to decide, naming me George Herbert Walker Bush.

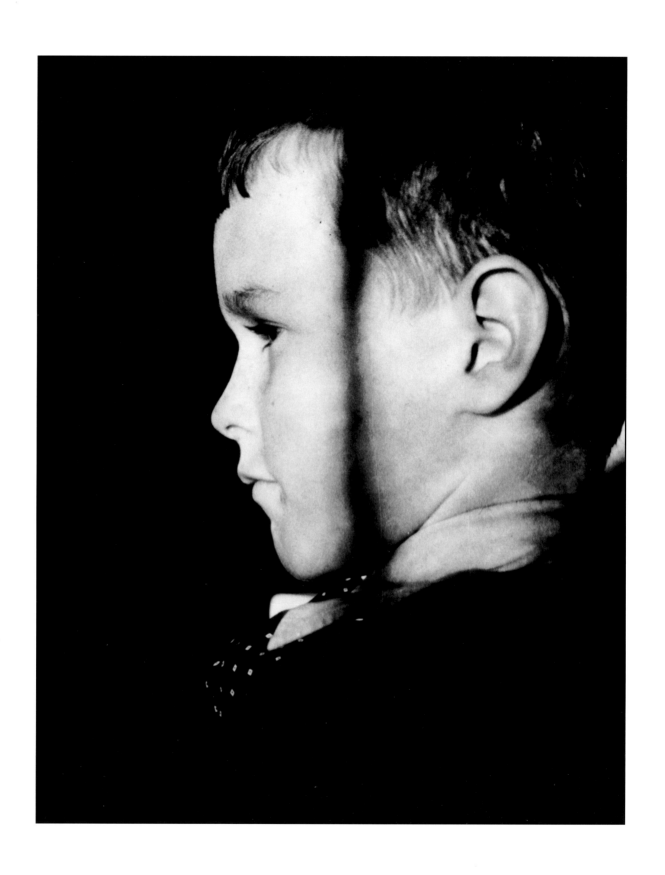

For the five Bush children growing up in Greenwich, Connecticut, our father had a powerful impact on the way we came to look at the world. But the writer who once described Dad as "the single greatest influence" on my life was only partly right. Our mother's influence and example were equally strong. Dad taught us about duty and service. Mother taught us about dealing with life on a personal basis, relating to other people.

Mother's criticism of her children, like dad's, was always constructive, not negative. They were our biggest boosters, always there when we needed them. They believed in an old-fashioned way of bringing up a family—generous measures of both love and discipline.

On my eighteenth birthday, I went to Boston and was sworn into the navy as Seaman Second Class. Not long thereafter, I was on a railway coach headed south for navy preflight training in North Carolina.

I was younger than the other trainees—the youngest aviator in the navy when I got my wings.

Like most TBM Avenger pilots, I liked the teamwork and camaraderie that went with being part of a three-man crew. I became attached to my plane, nicknaming it "Barbara."

Suddenly there was a jolt, as if a massive fist had crushed into the belly of the plane. Smoke poured into the cockpit, and I could see flames rippling across the crease of the wing, edging toward the fuel tanks. Still I was alive and had a chance. The question was whether my crew members had survived. Neither had responded after the order to bail out. Later I learned that neither Jack Delaney nor Ted White had survived.

I never got to meet Lou Gehrig, but one of the biggest moments my senior year came when his teammate, Babe Ruth, visited Yale to give the school library the original manuscript of his autobiography. It was the afternoon of our home game against Princeton, and as team captain, I took part in the pregame presentation ceremony. The ceremony was one of his last public appearances.

After a "secret" engagement, Barbara and I were married at her family church in Rye, New York, on January 6, 1945. I had just returned home after duty as a TBM Avenger aviator in the Pacific.

Breaking away meant just that—living on our own. I'd saved up three thousand dollars in the navy. Not much, but enough to get us started independently. We were young, still in our early twenties, and we wanted to make our own way, our own mistakes, and shape our own future.

The governor of Texas, George W. Bush

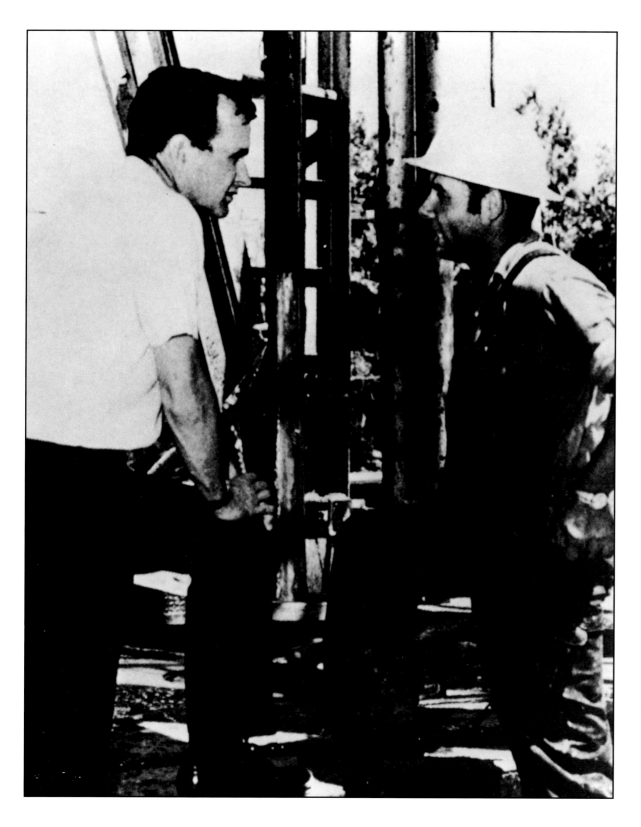

*A few years after World War II, I
started my own business. It was a
small business but not too small to
learn the facts of economic life in the
real American economy. I got my start
by taking a risk; I got my education
by making that company grow.*

In Midland I was bitten by the bug that led me into the oil business. Now I'd been bitten by another bug. In February, 1966, fifteen months after my unsuccessful race for the U.S. Senate, I resigned as chairman and CEO of Zapata to devote full time to running for Congress.

Johnson was president, and Time magazine reported, "It would be a blow to LBJ's personal vanity if his own home state were to elect Bush to join the Republican John Tower in an all-GOP Senate team."

Barbara shared my concern for the way things were going in the country and my feeling that we had an obligation to give something back to a society that had given us so much.

To Lincoln, the presidency helped play, as he put it, "America's mystic chords of memory." Shall we wait just one minute? And to Teddy Roosevelt, the presidency meant the "bully pulpit"—calling America's boundless energy. And it was Dwight Eisenhower, beloved Ike, who described its power "to proclaim anew our faith" and summon "lightness against the dark." To occupy this office is to feel a kinship with these and other presidents, each of whom in his own way sought to do right and, thus, to achieve good. Each summoned the best from the idea we call America; and each wondered, I suspect, how he could be worthy of God and man.

I owed Richard Nixon a great deal. . . . He came to Texas to campaign for me when I first got into elective politics, then gave me a rare opportunity to represent my country on an international level.

In later years, whenever I'd hear anyone make a slighting comment about President Ford's grasp of issues, I'd point out that in four years in Congress I'd never run into anyone who had a better grasp of the details of pending legislation than Jerry Ford when he was House Republican leader.

*The announcement of my appointment as
United Nations ambassador came December 11,
1970. Reaction started coming in immediately.
The news was well received on Capitol Hill.
When I reported to work as U.S. ambassador in
early March, 1971, after intense briefings, I had
no illusions about the U.N.'s limitations or my
role as America's chief representative at the "glass
palace." I was there as an advocate—not an
apologist for my country's policies.*

Barbara and I talked it over. We now agreed that if the president gave me a choice of overseas assignments, the thing to do was head for the Far East. An important, coveted post like London or Paris would be good for the resumé, but Beijing was a challenge, a journey into the unknown. A new China was emerging, and the relationship between the United States and the People's Republic would be crucial in the years to come, not just in terms of Asian but of worldwide American policy.

After Christmas recess, the full Senate approved the nomina-
tion by a 64–27 vote, and three days later my friend and
neighbor, Supreme Court Justice Potter Stewart, swore me
in as CIA director at the agency's headquarters in Langley,
Virginia, just across the Potomac from Washington.

America needed someone in the Oval Office who could restore the people's faith in our institutions, a leader who could revitalize the national spirit. By May 1, 1979, I announced my candidacy.

THE VICE PRESIDENTIAL YEARS

1981–1989

I recall sitting on the inaugural platform that clear, crisp day, January 20, 1981. The forecast had been for rain, but the sun broke through and the temperature was in the mid-fifties. The ceremonies took place, for the first time in history, on the west front of the Capitol, looking toward Pennsylvania Avenue. First, I took the oath of vice president, administered by my friend, Justice Potter Stewart, while Barbara held the family Bible; then there was a hymn, "Faith of our Fathers"; then Chief Justice Warren Burger administered the oath to the new president. There was a twenty-one gun salute, a pause, then Ronald Reagan spoke, pledging a stronger America, at peace, its economy revived, with renewed respect overseas and restored confidence here at home, an era of national renewal.

Welcome home for one of the Iranian hostages Bruce Langdon

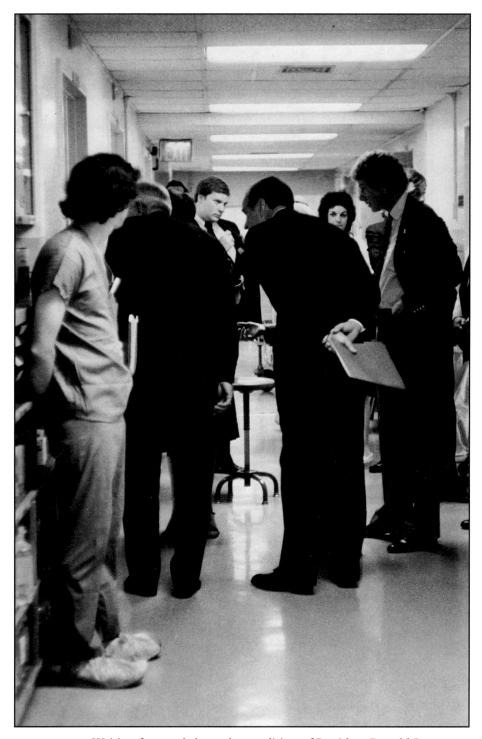

Waiting for word about the condition of President Ronald Reagan after assassination attempt

President Reagan's senior staff advising Vice President Bush

I'd been on the job only seventy days when the president was shot.

My relations with Ronald Reagan started out on a different footing. There was never a hint of negative feelings left over from our fight for the presidential nomination because Reagan's instinct, I learned, is to think the best of the people he works with. It was clear that once he'd made his decision on the vice presidency, he viewed the Reagan-Bush ticket not simply as a convenient political alliance but as a partnership. We would run and serve together as a team.

Dr. Martin Luther King was a crusader and an evangelist, who bore the weight of a pioneer. He was a force against evil. His life was a metaphor for courage. His goal was an America where equality and opportunity could coexist and where goodness could prevail. And through his courage, Dr. King changed America forever for the better.

A kinder, gentler environment also means a society where every man, woman, and child can live and prosper in an environment free from fear. And that, then, means freedom from crime.

We are a nation that was founded for liberty and human rights—for the freedom to speak and assemble and worship, each in our own way. This is our heritage—one that we must never abandon for the expediency of the moment.

Aboard *Air Force Two*

George W., Jeb, the vice president, Marvin, and Neil Bush as they appeared on the *Today* show

The 1984 Republican National Convention, Dallas, Texas

Geraldine Ferraro and I agreed on very few things in 1984, but we had a shared feeling that coverage of the vice presidential campaign lacked something. Still, I think the press does its job as well as it can, and I do mine as well as I can. I learned a great deal in that campaign. It's an adversarial relationship at times, but there's no reason it can't be between friendly adversaries.

Receiving concession phone call from Geraldine Ferraro

The friendship, the alliance between the United States and Israel is strong and solid— built upon a foundation of shared democratic values, of shared history and heritage that sustain the moral life of our two countries.

Democracy is on a roll in Latin America. Since we took office, the following countries have changed from military to democratic rule: Argentina, Ecuador, Peru, Honduras, Grenada, El Salvador, Brazil, Uruguay, and Guatemala. Ninety percent of the population of Latin America now lives under democracy.

Talking to President Duarte and on his left is Daniel Ortega of Nicaragua (Sandinista)

Deng Hsias Ping, The People's Republic of China

There's a Chinese proverb that says, "One generation plants a tree; the next sits in its shade." And there's a timeless wisdom in that. But thanks to your courageous reforms—and I don't minimize the difficulties—the Chinese people are planting great and sturdy trees, some of which are bearing fruit right now for this generation.

Summit Governor's Island, New York

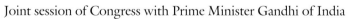
Joint session of Congress with Prime Minister Gandhi of India

Representing the president overseas—not only at state funerals but on special missions—is another facet of the modern vice presidency. From 1981 through the spring of 1987, I traveled to seventy-three foreign countries on presidential assignments both ceremonial and substantive.

The brutal and tragic horrors of Auschwitz serve as grim reminders of man's capacity for evil. The denial of human rights . . . leads ultimately to this, the attempted extermination of an entire people. Let us pledge our eternal vigilance that crimes of this magnitude will never happen again.

I seek the presidency for a single purpose, a purpose that has motivated millions of Americans across the years. . . . I seek the presidency to build a better America.

At home with the family in Kennebunkport, Maine

You go into public life hoping to secure the future for your children and the next generation. Then somewhere along the way, unless you're careful, you can overlook the fact that your first responsibility as a parent is to be there now, when your kids need you, while they're growing. Barbara and I were determined when we moved to Washington that we weren't going to forget our number one priority as parents.

Lauren, Barbara, and Marshall Bush

The Bush family, Walkers Point, Kennebunkport, Maine, summer of 1986

The modern vice presidency is the most misunderstood elective office in our political system. People either make too little or too much of it. Those who make too little of it see the office in premodern terms, as it existed before President Eisenhower upgraded the vice presidency, including Richard Nixon in the Cabinet and NSC meetings. Before Nixon, vice presidents weren't included in the White House decision making process. Their office was on Capitol Hill, and was considered in strict constitutional terms: the vice president's job, as long as the president was alive, was to preside over the Senate. Period.

I met Christa McAuliffe when she was at the White House. She was a teacher. I read out her name announcing her selection to a waiting country. She wanted to go into space because that's where the future is, and she wanted to tell her students about it. Christa McAuliffe never got a chance to tell us about space. But in the end she taught us about courage and grace, and she re-minded us that it's a good and fine thing to serve your country, and to serve the pursuit of knowledge. What a moving life and death.

I want to help more black Americans and other minorities experience the pride and dignity of ownership, of building something in the private sector.

Fishing buddy Ray Scott

This administration is profoundly committed to protecting
the environment that we all share.

One of the many campaign stops in Iowa

Millions of people are looking to America for the hope and encouragement they need as they seek the same freedom we have here—freedom of expression, security and opportunity we enjoy. And Americans will be there to help. But if America is to continue its traditional leadership role, we've got to be competitive enough to take on the job, and strong and smart enough to do it right.

Grandson Sam LeBlond on the campaign trail

Bush family support at campaign stop

A greeting for Michael Dukakis

Republican presidential candidates

Presidential debate with Michael Dukakis

Americans are better off today because we cut taxes, created jobs, and got this country's economy moving again. This administration took America from double-digit inflation to double-barreled recovery.

President Ronald Reagan, with Governor Pete Wilson *(far left)* and
Governor George Deukmejian *(right)*, supporting Vice President
George Bush in his run for the presidency

At the vice president's residence

Sleeping on *Air Force Two*

James Baker and Vice President Bush meet
with Senator Quayle in New Orleans

*The Congress will push me to raise taxes, and I'll say no,
and they'll push and I'll say no, and they'll push again,
and I'll say to them, "Read my lips: no new taxes."*

First campaign stop in Indiana with Senator Dan Quayle and family

Watching the election results in Houston, Texas

Practicing inaugural address at the Blair House in Washington, D.C., January 20, 1989

There is a man here who has earned a lasting place in our hearts and in our history. President Reagan, on behalf of our nation, I thank you for the wonderful things you have done for America.

THE PRESIDENTIAL YEARS

1989–1993

We meet on democracy's front porch. A good place to talk as neighbors and friends. For this is a day when our nation is made whole, when our differences, for a moment, are suspended. And my first act as President is a prayer. Heavenly Father, we bow our heads and thank You for Your love. Accept our thanks that yields this day and the shared faith that makes its continuance likely. Make us strong to do Your work, willing to heed and hear Your will, and write on our hearts these words: "Use power to help people." For we are given power not to advance our own purposes, nor to make a great show in the world, nor a name. There is but one just power, and it is to serve people. Help us to remember, Lord. Amen.

I've just repeated word for word the oath taken by George Washington two hundred years ago, and the Bible on which I placed my hand is the Bible on which he placed his. It is right that the memory of Washington be with us today not only because this is our bicentennial inauguration but because Washington remains the Father of our Country. And he would, I think, be gladdened by this day; for today is the concrete expression of a stunning fact: our continuity, these two hundred years since our government began.

Our principles are clear: that government service is a noble calling and a public trust.

Saying goodbye to the Reagans

Walking in the inaugural parade

I am privileged to be the president of the United States at this terribly exciting time not only in our history but in the history of freedom and democracy around the world.

First time in Oval Office as president—reading a note from former President Reagan

America today is a proud, free nation, decent and civil, a place we cannot help love. We know in our hearts, not loudly and proudly but as a simple fact, this country has meaning beyond what we see, and that our strength is a force for good.

Mrs. Dorothy Bush, mother of the president

You're talking about yourself too much, George,
mother said to me after a news report covering
one of my campaign speeches.

Pierce and Lauren Bush

Granddaughter Ellie LeBlond

All our hopes for our children will mean little if we don't make sure the education they're given is outstanding. The founders knew this—two hundred years ago they used to say: to plan for a decade, plant a tree, but to plan for a century, teach the children.

Grandsons Sam LeBlond and Jeb Bush

With Granddaughter Marshall and Millie on *Marine 1* helicopter

Outside the Oval Office with Lauren, Pierce, and Ashley Bush

The grandchildren at Kennebunkport, Maine

I've had some interesting jobs in my life, but not one of them was as interesting or demanding or frustrating or confusing or taxing . . . or as difficult as fatherhood, or parenthood, as they currently say, which is okay by me.

Millie

*A country founded on the concepts of freedom and fair play,
of honor and decency, relies on its public officials to live up to
those ideals, and not to abuse the trust the people have vested
in them.*

" . . . A presidency can shape an era—it can shape our lives.
A successful presidency can give meaning to an age. . . ."

The president's Cabinet prior to Senator John Tower's confirmation hearings

The president's Cabinet

The president's Cabinet

I remember the story of one group of boat people from Vietnam—they had survived brutality and famine in their own country, starvation, drowning and pirates in their leaking boat on the high seas, and when an American ship pulled along board they shouted to their rescuers, "Hello America. Hello freedom man."

The president with David Valdez and some of the Valdez family

. . . it's a pleasure to be back here in my home state of Texas . . . another hometown boy of whom I'm very proud: David Valdez, a Kingsville favorite son. He's a photo dog, we call him. He's the head photographer at the White House. I just met his family—that's the family that's filling up that whole bleacher over on that side there. So glad to see them.

With the press corps on *Air Force 1*

Senior White House staff Andy Card, Alixe Glen, and Robert Gates

With the press on the South Lawn of the White House

*Six nations in six months—and from six
different tongues we heard the same word: freedom. The people of Central Europe believed it.
They fought for it, and they deserve the credit.*

President Bush with former presidents at Richard Nixon's Presidential Library opening

Marlin Fitzwater, press secretary to Presidents Reagan and Bush, has all the presidents' attention

At the opening of the Ronald Reagan Presidential Library

First Lady Barbara Bush with former First Ladies Mrs. Reagan, Mrs. Johnson, Mrs. Nixon, Mrs. Carter, and Mrs. Ford

Talking to Marshall Bush in Oval Office

Promoting Barbara Bush's Literacy Program

*I am certain that God's help is absolutely
essential for anyone to lead this great
country of ours.*

Press conference in Kennebunkport

Like most Americans my age, I fought in combat in World War II, and I believe the best way to prevent a war is to maintain a strong and effective defense. That's my defense policy: peace through strength.

Oval Office meeting with National Security Advisors and Ranger

More than two hundred years ago, we secured democracy through the American Revolution, ensuring rights like freedom of speech, due process under the law, and to think and dream as we choose—also, I might add, the freedom to pray as we choose, which is why I support a constitutional amendment restoring voluntary prayer.

Left to right: James A. Baker III, Barbara Bush, George Bush, Raisa Gorbachev, Mikhail Gorbachev, Eduard Shevardnadze, Brent Scowcroft, and Marshal Akromeyev

As your President, I am determined to consult often with President Gorbachev to keep the door open to negotiation and peace. These indeed are exciting times, and I'm proud to be your president in these times of change.

In the Red Room in the White House with President Gorbachev

On the south lawn of the White House

At the Kremlin in Moscow

A hundred generations have searched for this elusive path to peace, while a thousand wars raged across the span of human endeavor. Today that new world is struggling to be born, a world quite different from the one we've known. A world where the rule of law supplants the rule of the jungle. A world in which the nations recognize the shared responsibility for freedom and justice. A world where the strong respect the rights of the weak. This is the vision I shared with President Gorbachev in Helsinki. He and other leaders from Europe, the Gulf, and around the world understand that how we manage the crisis today could shape the future for generations to come.

I've expressed my keen interest in seeing perestroika succeed. Gorbachev is the architect of perestroika. Gorbachev conducted the affairs of the Soviet Union with great restraint as Poland and Czechoslovakia and GDR (German Democratic Republic) and other countries achieved their independence. But you can't build a foreign policy of a country on the presence of an individual. You can build it on how you do facilitate the change toward democracy and freedom, whether it's in the countries where that's taken place or in the countries where it hasn't taken place. And so, I would say I salute the man for what he has done.

Felipe Gonzalez of Spain (left) and Mikhail Gorbachev at the Middle East Peace Conference in Barcelona, Spain

It is essential in these times of great change and great promise, and of major progress in arms control, that the community of nations works together even more diligently to prevent nuclear proliferation, which poses one of the greatest risks to the survival of mankind.

On a Soviet ship off the coast of Malta

With President Nelson Mandela

With President Asad of Syria in Geneva, Switzerland

I believe that America does have a special mission in the world; we are the flagship of freedom.

Camden Yards, Baltimore with Queen Elizabeth and
Prince Phillip

At Camp David with Prince Charles

Number 10 Downing Street with Margaret Thatcher

At the residence of President Lech Wałesa; below in Gdańsk, Poland

On April 5, 1989, Poland took its first steps towards its democratic destiny. For the first time in more than forty years in Eastern Europe, a people's voice would speak in free elections. Here in our country, we celebrate the Revolution of 1776; but we remember April 19, 1775, the day the revolution began, the day the "shot heard round the world" was fired in Lexington, Massachusetts. In your country, Poles will always remember April 5, the dawn of the revolution of '89. The revolution that began in Poland touched off a chain reaction that changed Europe and the world. Those two revolutions share a common aim that unites our two nations in the cause of freedom.

First in Poland, then across Eastern Europe—one nation after another broke the stranglehold of the state and embraced democracy. And here in our own hemisphere, in Panama and Nicaragua, the day of the dictator gave way to the decade of democracy. These transforming events brought freedom to tens of millions of people, and with that freedom, new challenges—digging out from under the wreckage of ruined economies, reclaiming rights and freedom long denied. Everywhere from Prague to Panama City, the time has come to make a start in the difficult work of democracy building.

Latin American presidents

Like all wars, we must be united in our efforts as a country and as a community. Parents, teachers, children, law enforcement officials must join as one. Business, labor, the professions—all must be a part of this crusade for a drug-free America.

The Pope in the Vatican

In this century, we've learned a painful truth about the monumental evil that can be done in the name of humanity. We've learned how a vision of utopia can become a hell on earth for millions of men and women. We've learned, through hard experience, that the only alternative to tyranny of man is the rule of law. That's the essence of our vision for Europe: a Europe where not only are the dictators dethroned but where the rule of law, reflecting the will of the people, ensures the freedom millions have fought so hard to gain.

Prime Minister Benazir Bhutto of Pakistan

President Mubarak of Egypt

The re-emergence of Egypt as a respected leader of the Arab world attests to President Mubarak's statesmanship and ability, as well as to Egypt's wisdom in pursuing the path of peace.

President Salinas of Mexico at the White House

Tiananmen Square, People's Republic of China

The relationship with Mexico is very important. We must never take it for granted. We've got the East-West equation and we have the Pacific Rim, but as I look at the world, we must never neglect our own friends in this hemisphere, in our front yard.

"Let my people go." Those were the words Moses spoke nearly four thousand years ago, when the Israelites took the first step on the march from captivity to freedom. All Americans share in the solemn pride of millions of Jewish men, women, and children everywhere as they commemorate the Exodus. It was a journey of courage and strength toward the dream of a better tomorrow. And today, as well, people all throughout the world have continued that epic journey, a quest for a new life of liberty and peace. We support them in their struggle for democracy, we admire them for their strength of conviction, and we pray for their success.

Prime Minister Shamir of Israel

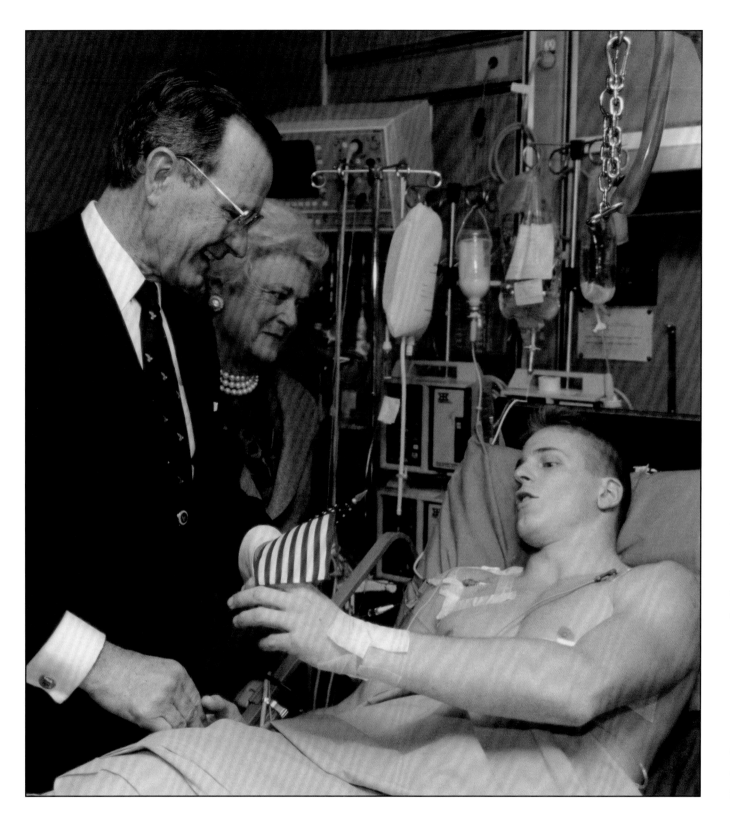

. . . on Wednesday, December 20, I ordered U.S. troops to Panama with four objectives: to safeguard the lives of American citizens, to help restore democracy, to protect the integrity of the Panama Canal treaties, and to bring General Manuel Noriega to justice. All these objectives have now been achieved.

I think America needs a human life amendment, and I
think when it comes to abortion there's a better way, the way
of adoption, the way of life.

State of the Union Address

Coretta Scott King

Texas has always had its share of pioneers and visionaries. One was Sam Houston. Where others saw empty plains and dust, he saw farms and ranches and towns. Where others saw obstacles, he saw opportunity. But Houston could scarcely have imagined that little more than one hundred years after his death, the entire planet would hold its breath as his name became the first word ever uttered on the plains and dust of another world. . . . It was July 20, 1969. And although Apollo 11 had just survived the most harrowing landing in the history of space, the voice of Neil Armstrong was confident, strong, American. He said, "Houston: Tranquility Base here. The Eagle has landed." Eight words . . . and the world was changed forever.

Space shuttle astronauts

Receiving notification in Aspen, Colorado of the Iraqi invasion of Kuwait

Standing up for our principles is an American tradition. As it has so many times before, it may take time and tremendous effort, but most of all, it will take unity of purpose. As I've witnessed throughout my life in both war and peace, America has never wavered when her purpose is driven by principle.

We stand at a unique and extraordinary moment. The crisis in the Persian Gulf, as grave as it is, also offers a rare opportunity to move toward an historic period of cooperation. Out of these troubled times, a new world order, can emerge: a new era—freer from the threat of terror, stronger in the pursuit of justice, and more secure in the quest for peace.

Camp David briefing

The United States is engaged in a collective effort, involving the overwhelming majority of the member states of the United Nations, to reverse the consequences of Iraqi aggression. Our goals, enshrined in five Security Council resolutions, are clear: the immediate and unconditional withdrawal of Iraqi forces from Kuwait; the restoration of Kuwait's legitimate government; the stability of Saudi Arabia and the Persian Gulf; and the protection of American citizens.

Ambassadors from the coalition countries supporting President Bush's Desert Storm initiatives, Prince Bandar of Saudi Arabia *(left)* and Ambassador Saud al Sabah *(right)*

Oval Office briefing by Colin Powell

Discussing military strategy using a map from *Time* magazine

We seek the immediate, unconditional, and complete withdrawal of all Iraqi forces from Kuwait.

The invasion of Kuwait was without provocation. The invasion of Kuwait was without excuse. And the invasion of Kuwait simply will not stand.

To preserve the peace, America will always stand for what's right. To preserve her commitments, America will always stand by her friends.

In the Oval Office with the Imir of Kuwait

Left to right: John Sununu, Brent Scowcroft, Bob Gates, and Marlin Fitzwater in the White House Press Briefing Room

We succeeded in the struggle for freedom in Europe because our allies remained stalwart. Keeping the peace in the Middle East will require no less. We're beginning a new era. This new era can be full of promise, an age of freedom, a time of peace for all peoples. But if history teaches us anything, it is that we must resist aggression or it will destroy our freedoms.

Recent events have surely proven that there is no substitute for American leadership. In the face of tyranny, let no one doubt our staying power. We will stand by our friends. One way or another, the leader of Iraq must learn this fundamental truth.

With U.S. troops in Saudi Arabia

Our objectives in the Persian Gulf are clear, our goals defined and familiar: Iraq must withdraw from Kuwait completely, immediately, and without condition.

A puppet regime imposed from the outside is unacceptable. The acquisition of territory by force is unacceptable. No one, friend or foe, should doubt our desire for peace; and no one should underestimate our determination to confront aggression.

Thanksgiving with the troops in Saudi Arabia during Desert Shield

Oval Office briefing on Kuwait

Less than a week ago, in the early morning hours of August 2, Iraqi Armed Forces, without provocation or warning, invaded a peaceful Kuwait.

Secretary of State Jim Baker in Oval Office briefing

In the president's study off the Oval Office with Colin Powell, Robert Gates, and Vice President Quayle watching
Foreign Minister Aziz of Iraq on television

In the life of a nation, we're called upon to define who we are and what we believe. Sometimes these choices are not easy. But today as president, I ask for your support in a decision I have made to stand up for what's right and condemn what's wrong in the cause of peace.

At my direction, elements for the 82nd Airborne Division as well as key units of the United States Air Force are arriving today to take up defensive positions in Saudi Arabia.

I thank God for the faith he's given me. And as I grow older I'm more aware of the spiritual element in life, and I ask for God's help.

The final decision to commit the U.S. military to combat in Desert Storm

The moment the bombing started in Baghdad

Monitoring the situation on CNN

Notification to Congressional leadership

The president's Cabinet in prayer for the safety of the U.S. military involved in action in Desert Storm

America not only is divinely blessed,
America is divinely accountable.

Meeting at Camp David

One of the many meetings that took place during Desert Shield and Desert Storm

Listening to a radio broadcast from Saddam Hussein as played on CNN

National Security Advisors

Gen. Colin Powell in the White House briefing on Desert Storm

General Powell on phone to Gen. Norman Schwarzkopf just a few hours before the end of the Gulf War

Kuwait is liberated. Iraq's army is defeated. Our military objectives are met. Kuwait is once more in the hands of Kuwaitis. . . .

In Washington, D.C., General Schwarzkopf leads the troops home

In South Carolina, greeting two pilots who had been shot down over Iraq

Fishing with Bob Bolard

With daughter Doro Koch

I believe in clean air and clean water and the protection of American wildlife. I also want to see our nation's public lands preserved so that this generation and future generations can use and enjoy our national bounty: the great outdoors.

Ted Williams and Joe DiMaggio

Michael Jackson

Rush Limbaugh and Roger Ailes

In Kennebunkport, Maine

I am very pleased to announce that I will nominate Judge Clarence Thomas to serve as Associate Justice of the United States Supreme Court.

People from far and wide, from all walks of life, all levels of education and income, have come here today in testament to the character of Clarence Thomas. But what brought you here is also something more: the power of the American ideal; the values of faith and family, of hard work and opportunity. These are the values that unite us all, that give America meaning.

Clarence and Mrs. Thomas with Justice White

The president and Ranger, one of Millie's pups, in Kennebunkport

In this more peaceful time, when our armies can become smaller, we must mold a world where the armies of people—people helping others—can become bigger, using what has been given to us, freedom and opportunity, to give back of ourselves. Through the adventure of community service, we can unlock new frontiers of empowerment, joining hands and linking hearts to further the work of God and man.

My feeling was and is that nothing beats personal, eye-to-eye contact in a political campaign—not just talking to or at people, but listening to what they have to say.

Think for a minute about the world we've already seen, a world of change: the Berlin Wall down; millions of people around the world took the first breath of freedom; and America, her ideals and her strengths intact, won the Cold War. That is good for every American.

They say this election is about change. Well, they're right. But let's not forget the things that must guide change are the things that never change: our belief in a strong defense, in strong families, and in leaving the world a better and more prosperous place for the young kids here today. That's what this election is about.

America is still the land of dreams, dreams as vast and wide as those plains out there in West Texas. Our dream, our ideals, our ideas have awakened dreams from Managua, to our south, all the way to Moscow. With faith in our people, we will reawaken those dreams right here in the United States of America.

The grandchildren, Camp David

Campaign '92

Just prior to the presidential debate, neither candidate was aware of the other's proximity

Presidential debate

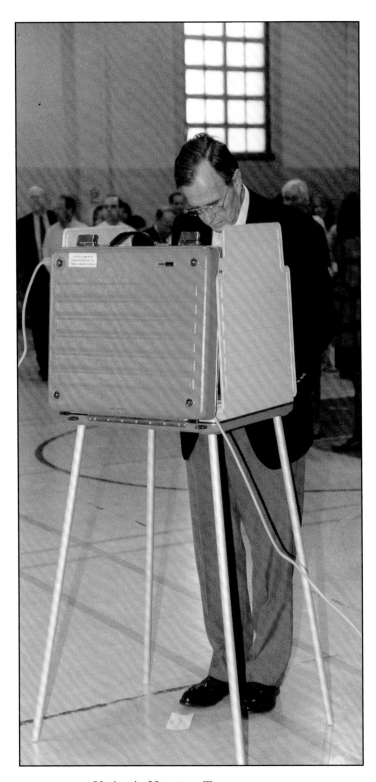

Voting in Houston, Texas

The Bush family watching the election results

President Bush writing his concession speech to Bill Clinton in Houston, Texas

Concession phone call to President-Elect Bill Clinton

*Way back in 1945, Winston Churchill was defeated at the
polls. He said, "I have been given the Order of the Boot."
That is the exact same position in which I find myself today.*

The people of Somalia, especially the children of Somalia, need our help. We're able to ease their suffering. We must help them live. We must give them hope. America must act.

With the Quayles on the last full day in the White House

A word about the vice president: Nobody could have asked to have a better vice president at his side than I had with Dan Quayle. He has been absolutely superb. Dan, I will be eternally grateful to you, and I just wish you all the best in the future.

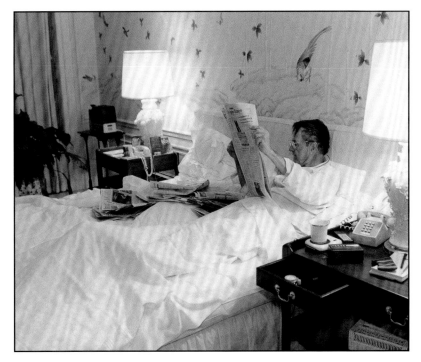

On the day of the inauguration, January 20, 1993

I am certain that God's help is absolutely essential for anyone to lead this great country of ours.

Don't worry about the Bushes. We are looking ahead now. And, we'll count our blessings when we get back to Houston on January 20 for all the friends that have supported us so much. God bless you all.

*I leave the White House grateful for
what we have achieved and also
exhilarated by the promise of what
can come to pass.*

On January 20, Barbara and I will head back to Texas. For us there will be no more elections, no more politics. But we will rededicate ourselves to serving others because, after all, that is the secret of this unique American spirit. With this spirit, we can realize the golden opportunity before us and make sure that our new day, like every American day, is filled with hope and promise.